Robert Brook

Elements of Style in Furniture and Woodwork

Robert Brook

Elements of Style in Furniture and Woodwork

ISBN/EAN: 9783337170837

Printed in Europe, USA, Canada, Australia, Japan

Cover: Foto ©ninafisch / pixelio.de

More available books at **www.hansebooks.com**

PREFACE.

LTHOUGH many books have been published with a view of illustrating various phases of Art manufacture, I am not acquainted with any work which presents in a concise form the characteristic details of the different styles of domestic furniture.

Feeling myself, the want of such an easily accessible hand-book, and believing that it will be equally useful to many others, both designers and manufacturers, I have endeavoured in the following series of sketches, in some measure to supply the deficiency.

It is, of course, impossible in a work of moderate dimensions, to give more than a selection from each period. I have, therefore, only chosen those examples which I have thought to be typical or suggestive, and likely to be of practical value to designers, avoiding any which possess only an antiquarian interest.

The importance of a knowledge of style being universally admitted, no apology need, I think, be offered for the publication of these drawings. They are intended chiefly for the use of those who, either from lack of time or opportunity, are prevented from consulting the numerous old authorities in woodwork, or examining the original specimens contained in our art galleries and museums. The enlarged details of mouldings, carvings, iron and brass mounts, &c., should also be serviceable to manufacturers who wish to reproduce cabinet work in any particular style.

As regards the relative merits of the various schools of design represented in the following pages, each one must judge for himself; there being no fixed laws by which to decide matters of taste. There are few styles which do not contain some elements worthy of imitation, and most of them offer valuable suggestions to the designer.

At no period in the world's history has a knowledge of the decorative and constructive Arts as practised by various nations, been so universal as it is at present. One result of this spread of information is, that we have no prevailing style of our own, but reproductions of the works of all ages and countries, modified to suit modern requirements. Some draw their inspirations from Gothic forms, others are guided by Classic models, and others again prefer to adapt one of the many varieties of Oriental Art. With this diversity of taste, a national style is impossible, nor can we hope for any great perfection when the energies of our architects and designers are distributed over such a wide field of study.

This was not the case in the great Art periods of former times, when the talents of many generations of Art-workers were combined for the perfection of a single style.

A fickle public now demands something "fresh" every few years, and change of fashion in architecture and furniture is almost as rapid as change of fashion in dress. The chief aim of the Ancients was to improve on existing types, and not to produce novel effects, and it is to this unity of purpose we may attribute all the great works of antiquity—the Grecian Temples and Gothic Cathedrals, the models from which all subsequent European styles have sprung, and on which all future variations must be founded. But although we cannot hope to improve on the proportions of the antique, or excel it in purity of design, we can at least avoid those incongruities which characterise the most debased periods of Art, by obtaining as much knowledge as possible of the styles in which we wish to work, and noticing the peculiarities by which the productions of every age and country are distinguished. All good authorities are of opinion that an acquaintance with the works of the great masters in Architecture and Design is advantageous, in fact essential, to those who wish to adopt either of the above professions. As Owen Jones truly remarks in his preface to the Grammar of Ornament, "To attempt to build up theories of Art or to form a style independently of the past, would be an act of supreme folly. It would be at once to reject the accumulated knowledge of thousands of years." At the same time we should not slavishly copy old examples, but examine them with the object of discovering the methods which their originators adopted, and use them as "motifs" on which to graft original thought.

ROBERT BROOK.

ITALIAN RENAISSANCE.

Plates 1 to 7.

I T is difficult to fix the precise date when Gothic, or geometrical, forms gave place to the more naturalesque treatment which characterised the Renaissance in Italy; but it is certain that the change above mentioned commenced some time between the years 1400 and 1450.

The commencement of the fifteenth century witnessed a great revival in the study of classical literature, and there is no doubt that this circumstance had a considerable influence on the architectural and decorative arts of the period. The constant discovery of many beautiful remains of antiquity in various parts of Italy about this time also tended to foster a taste for the old methods and symbols of ornamentation, which had possibly only lain dormant during the intervening centuries, or Gothic period, waiting to be once more developed. Once started, the new fashion spread very rapidly, and was adopted with enthusiasm by many architects and artists of eminence, the results of whose labours are to be seen in the glorious palaces, churches, and cathedrals scattered over the length and breadth of Italy.

In the fifteenth and sixteenth centuries the number of pieces of household Furniture in general use was extremely limited. The chief articles were: Tables, either consisting of simple boards fastened on trestles, or moulded tops resting on carved or turned supports; Chairs with solid backs, carved in high relief; and Chests or Coffers, either carved in hard wood and polished, or carved and gilt, and sometimes still further enriched with painting. Many fine examples of these Chests are still extant, in a perfect state of preservation. On plate 4 will be found portions of two in the South Kensington Museum, which is very rich in specimens of this important piece of Renaissance Furniture.

These Chests, or Marriage Coffers as they are sometimes called, were used for containing clothes, tapestries, gold and silver plate, and other valuables, and were presented to the bride and bridegroom, with the other wedding gifts, on the occasion of their marriage. It was probably for this reason that so much skill and taste was lavished on their production. There are specimens at South Kensington, for instance, which are 6 ft. or 7 ft. long, and richly carved and gilt, the panels being painted with historical and other subjects, which must have cost originally very large sums of money.

One great feature in Italian Renaissance woodwork is the extreme delicacy and beauty of the carving with which it is generally embellished. Graceful scrolls and arabesques, birds, fruit and flowers, and the usual classical details, were all executed with consummate skill by the carvers of this period, as is proved by the numerous specimens of their handiwork remaining at the present day for our study and imitation.

Walnut and chestnut appear to have been the favourite woods in use at the time of which we write. They were probably chosen on account of their suitability for carving, which was then the almost universal method of enrichment.

Most of the examples sketched on sheets 1 to 7 are from pieces of Italian Furniture of the fifteenth and sixteenth centuries.

In making a selection of details from this and other styles that will be practically useful, the difficulty is not to find examples, but to choose typical specimens and such as are not over-enriched or covered with carving. Plain and simple pieces of fifteenth and sixteenth century Furniture are extremely scarce, for several reasons. In the first place, in early times, say down to the commencement of the seventeenth century, Furniture of the better sort was a comparative luxury, made principally for the nobility and upper classes ; and inferior or simple Furniture was, from its plain appearance, less taken care of, and subject to rougher usage than the costly examples which our museums contain, and being, of course, less carefully made, was unable to stand the destructive influences of time, and ordinary wear and tear. It is therefore difficult to obtain a correct idea of the Furniture in use among the middle classes previous to the sixteenth century.

On glancing over the Italian specimens at South Kensington, for instance, we see a variety of rich Chests, carved and gilt Chairs, Mirror Frames, Tripods, and fragments of internal woodwork, most of which are decorated with figures, devices, and armorial bearings, indicating that they once belonged to Italian princes and nobles ; but of the Furniture of an ordinary middle-class house we see absolutely nothing. This deficiency is much to be regretted, but, for the reasons above mentioned, it appears to be quite unavoidable. In the following sketches the least ornate specimens have been selected, as they will probably be found more useful to the majority of our subscribers.

In the carved panels shown on sheets 5 and 6 it will be noticed that delicate arabesques, birds, fruit, grotesque heads, and various other natural objects, were favourite subjects for imitation with Renaissance artists. In some cases their work shows a refinement of outline and delicacy of finish that have never been surpassed.

As we have previously remarked, it was Italy that first witnessed the dawn of Renaissance Art, and although the new style found many talented exponents in other countries, particularly in France, it is to Italy we must look for the purest and most refined examples. These, fortunately, are to be found in great abundance ; in fact there is hardly an Italian town of any importance that does not possess one or more public buildings containing specimens of carved Renaissance woodwork, generally in tolerable preservation.

The choir stalls, confessional boxes, and wall-panelling of the Italian churches are full of interest to the Furniture designer, and offer valuable suggestions for the treatment of Cabinets, Sideboards, Seats, and other articles of domestic use.

The variety of design displayed in Renaissance carving is almost unlimited, although the arabesque generally forms the groundwork for most of the schemes of panel and surface decoration. It was in the accessories to the scroll enrichments that the Italian artist showed his fertility and invention to the greatest advantage. He was here comparatively unfettered, and could let his imagination have full play. Birds, fruit, flowers, animals, human and grotesque figures, etc., etc., flowed from his hand apparently without effort, the result being a school of decorative design which has afforded models to successive generations of artists.

It is to the earlier Italian work, however, that the student will most profitably confine his attention, particularly that of the fifteenth and sixteenth centuries for at that time the ornamental details reached their greatest delicacy and perfection. Later on, in the seventeenth century, everything in the way of decorative art became clumsy and heavy.

In the consideration of an architectural style, it is impossible to attach too much importance to the various mouldings belonging to it. This remark applies with equal force to the various styles of Furniture and constructive woodwork, the mouldings of which invariably follow those in the Architecture of the period. This is particularly noticeable in the Renaissance work executed before the professions of architect and Furniture designer became distinct. In early times the architect designed the Cabinets and household Furniture as well as the buildings, and he used very similar mouldings for both stone and wood. Plate 2 is devoted entirely to Italian mouldings of various descriptions. Some of these were intended for execution in stone, but if carried out on a smaller scale they are equally suitable for wood.

The great resemblance between the Architectural and Furniture details of the fifteenth and sixteenth centuries proves beyond doubt that they may in many instances be attributed to the same hands. It is, indeed, a well known fact that artists and sculptors of the highest eminence did not formerly think it derogatory to devote their careful attention to the design and embellishment of articles of every-day use. This accounts for the high character of many objects now considered of minor importance, but which, at the time of their production, were evidently thought worthy of the greatest consideration. Even such small details as handles and lock-plates were carefully thought out and designed to harmonize with the Cabinets, etc., to which they were to be fixed. Good examples of Italian Furniture mounts are comparatively scarce. This may partly be accounted for by the fact that in the course of years many of them have become detached from the articles to which they originally belonged ; and it must also be remembered that the number of pieces of Renaissance Furniture embellished with metal handles and lock-plates of any importance has always been limited.

Most of the old Coffers, for instance, are devoid of handles, and show no traces of ever having had any ; so that they must have been lifted bodily whenever it was necessary to move them.

At that most interesting and instructive store-house of beautiful objects, the South Kensington Museum, a few fine specimens of Italian Cabinet and Drawer handles are preserved. Some of these appear on plate 7. They are mostly of bronze or hammered iron. The two pilasters on plate 5 have been taken from an old Italian frontispiece published at Venice in 1470. The complete design will be found on the title-page of this volume. It has been reproduced intact, with the exception that the author's name and date of publication have been inserted in the upper and lower panels, in place of the figures which they originally contained. The beautiful early Italian ornament in these pilasters has been slightly shaded in the sketch, so as to show its suitability for carving.

DESCRIPTION OF PLATES 1 TO 7,—ITALIAN RENAISSANCE.

PLATE

1.—Mirror Frame, Capitals, Pilasters, and carved Panels.

2.—Italian Mouldings.

3.—Pediments.

4.—Chair Support, carved Chests, Pedestal, and Turning.

5.—Carved Panels.

6.—Ditto.

7.—Handles and Lock Plates.

GERMAN RENAISSANCE.

T HE particular treatment of Renaissance details adopted by the Germans cannot be described as strictly original, but it presents certain points of difference from the Italian from which it was derived, and also from the French. German woodwork, although not equal either to the French or Italian in point of refinement, very often excels them both in richness of detail and facility of manipulation. There never was a period, probably, when the wood-carvers art reached such general perfection, and was so universally used, both for exterior and interior purposes, as in Germany, Belgium, and Flanders in the sixteenth and seventeenth centuries. Consequently, there are endless remains of domestic woodwork to be found all over those parts of the Continent. The chief difficulty is to select examples from such a mass of available material. For those who are unable to inspect the work " in situ," the designs of Vriedman de Vriese and Wendel Dietterlin may be profitably studied ; as they give a very good idea of the quaintness and fertility of invention displayed by German artists of the best period. The Tables on plate 8 are by de Vriese. They are distinguished by their solidity, and give evidence of a knowledge of sound constructive principles on the part of their designer.

The most characteristic German work dates from the sixteenth century, when the Italian influence was to a great extent outgrown, and the quaint, picturesque and sometimes humorous German feeling asserted itself. The examples on plates 8, 9, and 10, do not call for any special explanation. They are chiefly valuable as suggestions, and the numerous purposes to which they may be adapted will be at once apparent to practical men.

The piece at top of sheet 10 is in reality a centre Table of rather peculiar construction ; having cupboards and drawers beneath top. The general elevation of this might easily be adapted to a sideboard back, and the two fragments at bottom of sheet, which are portions of high dado panelling, would with very slight alteration make up into overdoors for the library or dining-room. The construction of Tables on sheets 8, 9, and 10 is also worth attention.

DESCRIPTION OF PLATES 8, 9, 10.—GERMAN RENAISSANCE.

PLATE.

8.—Two Chairs, Centre Table, Table Ends.

9.—Hanging Bookcase, Buffet, Table, Carved Panel.

10.—Centre Table, Table Ends, Portions of Wall Panelling.

ELIZABETHAN AND JACOBEAN.

THE impossibility, in many cases, of distinguishing between Elizabethan and Jacobean woodwork induces me to include them under the same heading. As a matter of fact, there are certain variations in detail which enable the experienced observer to state with tolerable accuracy to which of the above reigns pieces of "old oak" may be attributed, but there are many instances in which even the highest authorities are at fault, for the simple reason that the Elizabethan style of construction and ornamentation was continued far into the reign of James I. It is really towards the end of his reign that a more clearly defined alteration in style is observable. The construction becomes simpler and a more Italian feeling prevails, and the carved enrichments are introduced with a more sparing hand. Roughly speaking, the more ornate specimens are generally Elizabethan and the simpler and more severe ones Jacobean.

It would possibly be more correct to describe the style under notice as "English Renaissance," but here again the designation would not be perfectly correct, for although a revival of classical tastes actually took place in England about this time, it was not only introduced by foreigners (chiefly Italians and Dutchmen) but during many years, almost exclusively carried on and practised by them. It is true that a fine school of English Architects and Carvers eventually arose, but the initiative and early stages of development must be credited to foreign artists.

Gothic began to give place to classic forms in England at the commencement of the sixteenth century. Hans Holbein, the court painter, was one of the artists who exercised a great influence on decorative work at this time. His designs are almost purely Italian in character. This standard of purity was, unfortunately, not sustained by his successors, but allowed to degenerate into a coarseness of detail which cannot be commended by persons of cultivated tastes.

The great charm of Elizabethan woodwork is its picturesqueness and variety; much of this would, it must be admitted, be lost by a refining process; so that we must be content to take it for better or for worse, and admire its quaintness and originality where we can. There is no scarcity of examples of old oak in England fortunately. Every county possesses its ancestral Halls containing Furniture and constructive woodwork of more or less importance. Carved Chests, Bedsteads, Cupboards or Buffets, Chimney-Pieces, Chairs, Tables and Settles, generally darkened with age and very massive, still remain to remind us of the sturdy period in English history when the word "home" which has since become the most cherished in our language was first properly understood.

The turned legs on plate 11 are in our way of thinking, enormously heavy, but possibly not unnecessarily so considering they were made for much rougher times than our own. One reason for the want of finish observable in Elizabethan woodwork, may be attributed to the fact that in the early days of Furniture-making the distinctive trade of cabinet-maker was unknown. The builder, or village carpenter (sometimes in conjunction with the architect), executed the movables as well as the fitments that were required for the sixteenth and seventeenth century houses, and these worthy artists and workmen, being accustomed to timber construction on a large scale did not enter always into the minutiæ of cabinet-making, as we now understand it. At the present day fashions in Furniture are set in the large towns by artists, or associations of artists and manufacturers, and any novelty is rapidly circulated all over the country by means of illustrated journals, books, and local exhibitions, so that a country maker may easily keep pace with the times. Formerly things were far otherwise.

In the good old days new ideas filtered very slowly from the principal centres of invention, and consequently the local carpenter or builder was compelled to rely principally on his own resources. This was not an unmixed disadvantage ; for the individuality of the workman was by this means developed and unconsciously impressed on his work, in the shape of quaint and original conceits in carving and construction, which would probably have never occurred to him had he possessed books of reference or illustrated papers to refer to. Plate 12 shows some of the more ornamental specimens of Pilasters, Newels, supports to Chimney-pieces, &c., chiefly selected from Richardson's " Studies of old English Mansions," a most useful work for those who wish to gain a more comprehensive idea of old English Architecture, etc.

The quality of the carving to be found on Elizabethan Furniture varies considerably. In some cases it is almost equal to fine Italian work ; in others it is as coarse and primitive in design as the ornament on an Indian War Club or Canoe. This difference will be noticed in the examples on plate 13. The three lower panels here shown, which belong to what we should term the carpenter's version of Elizabethan, although effective in appearance, are wanting in finish and refinement, and they are also weak in the drawing of the details. The central panel on same sheet is of a higher class altogether, and shows considerably more knowledge of design.

The carver who executed this panel was probably a foreigner or an English workman who had studied abroad. The original from which the sketch was made is on some old woodwork from a house near Exeter, acquired by the South Kensington authorities and at present to be seen in one of the Furniture Courts of the Museum. The date of this woodwork is about 1600 to 1620. Plate 13 also contains examples of the interlaced strapwork style of ornamentation so characteristic of this period. The pattern is formed by sinking the ground-work about a quarter of an inch below the surface, leaving the face of the board or panel of a uniform height all over. Sometimes the ground was punched, probably to hide the irregularities of the surface. There is an almost infinite variety of designs of this class, both in wood and stone ; some of them of a very elaborate description. Elizabethan carvers were also very fond of introducing coats of arms with the edges of the shields very much cut up and twisted, and sometimes surrounded with the strapwork just mentioned.

A similar class of design, but executed in plaster on a much larger scale, is to be found on the ceilings of the sixteenth and seventeenth century houses.

Plate 14 shows a variety of Elizabethan mouldings, some plain and others enriched. They are Italian in character, but coarser, and a trifle less correct in proportion. They have been taken principally from Chimney-Pieces and Buffets, of which there are a great number of examples in this country. Interesting pieces of old woodwork are often to be found in country churches in the shape of pulpits, pew doors, wall panelling, chests, &c. It is only in remote districts, however, that pews dating from the period under notice remain in their original condition. The Chimney Piece was the most conspicuous feature in the Elizabethan interior, and on it the Architect and Carver lavished a considerable amount of thought and skill. As a rule, the lower portion, that is from the mantel shelf downwards, was of stone or marble, occasionally alabaster, and the upper part was generally made of wood. When not carved with a coat of arms or some other heraldic device, the principal panel was frequently filled with a portrait of some member of the family to which the house belonged. In the less important rooms the space above shelf was simply panelled or divided into unequal spaces, by pilasters supporting cornice mouldings. Examples of this type of chimney-piece will readily occur to our readers, as they are to be found in most country towns and cathedral cities, either in the old inns, or in the Squire's Hall or family mansion. The more elaborate chimney-pieces are surmounted with pediments varying in design with the style of the general fittings of the room. In some cases they were simple mouldings, architecturally grouped ; in others it was customary to pierce (or fret cut as we now call it) a flat board, the portion not cut away forming a pattern of interlaced scrolls and bars, similar to examples shown on plate 15. The exteriors of many of the buildings at the commencement of the seventeenth century were also frequently decorated with this style of ornament, but on a much larger scale and in stone. This class of work has a very "gingerbread" effect, but as it is characteristic of the Style, we feel bound to draw attention to it.

Plate 16 consists of drawer, handle, and lock plates. Although specimens of Elizabethan metal work of this class are not rare, it requires considerable search to bring together many that may be correctly termed representative examples, there being such a great similarity between much of the wrought-iron work executed in Elizabeth's reign and that produced previously. The old Gothic feeling, in fact, did not die out until long after the introduction of the Renaissance. An examination of the handles, &c., on plate 16, will show the influence of the previous style very clearly. In almost every case hammered iron was the material used for Furniture mounts at the end of the sixteenth and beginning of the seventeenth century. Brass did not come into general use for this purpose until nearly 100 years later.

DESCRIPTION OF PLATES 11 to 16.—ELIZABETHAN & JACOBEAN.

PLATE

11.—Turned Legs, Balusters, Finials, &c.

12.—Pilasters, Newels, Portions of Carved Chimney Pieces.

13.—Carved Panels, chiefly from Chests and Interior Woodwork.

14.—Mouldings.

15.—Pediments from Chimney Pieces, Overdoors and Chair Backs.

16.—Handles and Lock Plates.

LOUIS XIV.

FRENCH Furniture reached the highest degree of splendour and magnificence at the time of Louis XIV. It was in the reign of that sumptuous monarch that the palace at Versailles was completed ; and as he desired to fill its spacious galleries with Furniture that would rival their decoration in richness, he commissioned numerous talented artists, under the direction of Lebrun, to prepare designs for the various articles required, apparently without any regard to expense. The principal object appears to have been to produce something as striking and gorgeous in appearance as possible ; and that they succeeded in their efforts in that direction is fully proved by the numerous elaborate pieces of Furniture which have come down to us from this period. The names, also, of many of the designers and art workmen who assisted in producing these costly specimens of cabinet work, are preserved, although it is impossible in some cases to identify the handiwork of each master. The artists who figured most prominently in connexion with the design or manufacture of Furniture in Louis XIV.'s reign were Jean and Claude Berain, Lepautre, also a great decorative designer, Daniel Marot, and André Charles Boule, the last-mentioned the inventor of the class of work inlaid with tortoiseshell and brass which bears his name. Many fine pieces of Boule Furniture are in this country. Her Majesty the Queen has several at Windsor Castle ; so has Sir Richard Wallace ; and one of the finest is a grand Armoire that was presented to the South Kensington Museum, with other choice pieces of French Furniture, by the late Mr. John Jones, of Piccadilly. This single piece has been valued at £10,000. It was probably designed by Jean Berain, who excelled all his contemporaries in his particular branch, and he may be taken as the best exponent of the Louis XIV. style as regards cabinet work. The designs of Daniel Marot are sometimes very good, but they are more clumsy than Berain's ; and the same objection must be taken to those of Lepautre, although the decorative work of this artist is justly admired.

As previously remarked, the chief characteristic of Louis XIV. Furniture is magnificence, and it would therefore be quite out of place if introduced in an ordinary small dwelling. It requires costly surroundings, and is essentially a style suitable for a palace—not for a cottage. From a constructive point of view, Furniture of this period is often open to serious objections ; but it is undoubtedly the most suitable that could have been placed in the apartments for which it was originally intended. As is the case with other styles, it faithfully reflects the characteristics of the age, which was one of glitter and display, in strong contrast with the ultra-refinement and delicacy which prevailed later on, during the reign of Louis XVI.

The examples on plate 17 represent legs and other supports to Tables, the two lower ones being Clock Stands. They are chiefly from designs by Jean Berain, and the enrichments would in most cases be of carved wood, gilt, or chased brass, mounted on a groundwork of ebonized wood.

It must not be inferred from the foregoing remarks on Louis XIV. Furniture that it is to be condemned *in toto ;* on the contrary, it has many very excellent qualities. In the first place, it is original ; being unlike anything that had previously appeared ; and it is also generally vigorous in design, and rarely disfigured by the flimsy and meaningless ornament which is to be found on much of the Furniture made during the following reign. When to these good qualities are added the high finish and extreme beauty of the metal mounts with which Louis XIV. Furniture was frequently embellished, it must be admitted that it is a style deserving the careful attention of the modern designer and manufacturer of Furniture. Although, if properly produced, this class of work can never be cheap, yet it is possible, by studying its peculiarities, to produce, in a modified form, many useful pieces of Furniture that would be within the bounds of modern expenditure.

The examples on plate 18 are from designs by Berain, Paul Decker, and Daniel Marot. The two portions of Cabinets at top are by Berain, the centre glass and two side pilasters by Paul Decker, who, although he was not a Frenchman, seems to have been thoroughly imbued with the feeling of the period. The two sketches at bottom of sheet represent a Bracket and Stand for a Clock, by Daniel Marot.

In all periods of Decorative art, certain lines, or combinations of lines, will be found to occur more frequently than others. As this predominance or repetition of lines gives, to a great extent, a character to the work of any period, and stamps the date of its production, it is most important, in order to properly understand a style, to find out the distinctive line or lines dominating it. In Gothic architecture and its accessories, the main lines were almost invariably geometrical, or, in other words, they could have been produced with a compass and T square, without the direct employment of the hand. The designs of the window tracery and screenwork, for instance, are mostly made up of numerous segments of circles struck from various centres, in combination with straight lines. Most of these could have been set out by any one possessing sufficient knowledge of the use of instruments, and with a certain amount of ingenuity. Not so with Italian work ; the Renaissance artists, on the contrary, relied chiefly on the free use of the hand for the formation of the patterns which were to enrich wood, stone, and metal. In the fifteenth and sixteenth centuries, a flowing line, unbroken by any sudden curves, runs through and forms the backbone of all the best ornament—a line similar, in fact, to Hogarth's line of beauty. In the eighteenth century we find a curve, certainly, but it is often used to excess, broken, and twisted in a variety of meaningless scrolls, without reason or motive. This is especially observable in French work dating from the end of the reign of Louis XV. In the reign of Louis XIV. a far truer appreciation of the correct principles of design existed, as it was understood that no piece of decorative art should consist entirely of either straight or curved lines, but that they should be used together, the one to relieve or accentuate the other. As a result of this knowledge put into practice, we have many beautiful examples of panels, friezes, pilasters, and other details with which all who are acquainted with the period in question are familiar. A straight line or bar, or a series of bars interlaced, and terminating with scrolls, is a distinguishing characteristic of Louis XIV. ornamentation. We find this method of enrichment introduced in the form of inlays of wood and brass in the Cabinet Furniture, and also painted and carved on the walls of apartments. Most of the examples on page 21 contain the combination of straight and curved lines we have mentioned.

The characteristic pediment with head in centre, at top of page 19, is the upper portion of a glass frame, very boldly carved and perforated. The pedestal on left is inlaid in the style of Boule, and the one on the right would be carved in oak. Most of the Cabinet Furniture of this period which was not of oak was either carved and gilt, or ebonized, and inlaid with brass and tortoiseshell, as above mentioned. Furniture was not lacking, either of a useful or an ornamental description. The seats were, as a rule, very large and roomy, and upholstered in rich silk, velvet, or embroidery. Chairs and Settees with high square backs and carved scroll arms, and stretchers; lofty Beds hung with heavy draperies; massive Tables supported on legs similar to those sketched on sheet 17; Cabinets, Pedestals, Screens, and Footstools, —helped to fill the apartments at this luxurious period; while the walls were adorned with Brackets supporting Clocks, Mirrors, and Candelabra. Those who are unable to cross the Channel to inspect Louis XIV. interiors, furnished in the manner we have described, may obtain some idea of their magnificence on a smaller scale by visiting the State apartments at Hampton Court. Much of the "Queen Anne" Furniture to be found there bears a very strong resemblance to the French work manufactured during the reign of the "Grand Monarque."

The Screen on sheet 20 is given in Jacquemart's useful History of Furniture. The frame, which is boldly carved, and gilt, surrounds a handsome panel, the pattern being formed by an embroidery of various-coloured beads. The caps and pilasters on same sheet will be found in the grand work of Jean Berain, a copy of which is in the Art Library at South Kensington Museum.

Lepautre's designs for Furniture are, as a rule, on far too grandiose a scale for ordinary purposes; they will, however, be found to contain excellent examples of the handsome mouldings for which the Louis XIV. style is distinguished. Lepautre, who was born in Paris in 1618, commenced his artistic career as an architect, designer, and engraver, shortly after the death of Louis XIII. He has, in some cases, been classed with the masters of that school; but this is a mistake, as he was essentially a representative, and one of the principal ones, of the period under notice.

The number of architectural, ornamental, and other designs, published by this prolific artist was enormous, and they are now justly esteemed by collectors and students, both on account of their intrinsic merit, and also as being historically interesting, illustrating, as they do, a sumptuous period of French Art.

Most of the mouldings represented on sheet 21 have been taken from old engravings by Lepautre; the remainder are from the works of his contemporary Berain.

In considering the Louis XIV. style of furnishing, the brass mounts must not be overlooked, as they are important and noticeable features on most of the Cabinet Furniture of the time. They are generally boldly conceived, and modelled with great skill. Sometimes the ormolu mounts almost cover the surface of the legs and Cabinet fronts. In fact, robbed of these metallic accessories, many of the articles would lose their greatest attraction. In Boule work, especially, the actual wood plays but a secondary part in the construction, and is merely the background on which the handsome chased brass ornamentation is displayed. The examples given comprise several details of " Boule " Furniture, and as we do not think a large variety of highly-chased and inimitable brasswork would be of much practical value to modern cabinet-makers, a few typical lock-plates and handles only are shown, drawn to an increased scale, on sheet 22. The large drop handle at bottom of page has been sketched from one of a set in possession of the author. These have evidently, at some former time, been attached to a Commode or Bureau. The actual width of the handle, over all, measures 11 inches; so that a Chest of Drawers mounted with a set of handles of this pattern, richly gilt, with key-plates to match, must have presented a very handsome appearance, and would hardly have required much additional embellishment.

DESCRIPTION OF PLATES 17 TO 22.—LOUIS XIV.

LOUIS XV.

T the expiration of the reign of Louis XIV. a marked change in ornamental design took place in France. To satisfy the cravings of an enervated and frivolous community, some new fashion had to be adopted, and the artists and architects of the period seem to have pandered without hesitation to the prevailing bad taste. This change of style, however, was not effected suddenly ; the characteristics of Louis XIV.'s work were gradually blended with a less severe and more curvilinear method of enrichment. The Louis XV. style can, in fact, be divided into two phases ; the earlier is generally known as " Regence " (from the fact of its having developed during the Regency of the Duke of Orleans), the later as " Rococo." The principal exponents of the former phase are Gilles Marie Oppenort and Pineau, whose works on Interior Decoration and Furniture should be consulted by those who wish to become thoroughly acquainted with " Louis Quinze " in its initial stages of development. In the Regence period there was a certain reserve and moderation observed in the designs, and straight lines were judiciously blended with agreeable curves ; but in a few years all restraint was abandoned, and in the ornamentation, as in the manners of the time unbridled license prevailed. We find extravagant twists and scrolls strung together in a meaningless manner and without any regard to propriety, even the two sides of a piece of Furniture in some cases not being alike. So called ornament is made to serve the part of construction, and ponderous structures are found resting on only scrolls and shells and foliage, spiky twists, birds, and human figures are mixed up in inextricable confusion. That there should be persons of cultivated tastes who admire the Furniture of this later period must always be a matter of astonishment to those who believe in one of the first principles of design, viz., " that construction should be ornamented, not ornament constructed." We can only account for this apparent perversion of taste by the fact that all this folly and extravagance was partially redeemed by the surprising skill of the metal-workers and chasers who executed the brass mounts with which the cabinets, etc., were so lavishly adorned. In these we can find much to admire, robbed of them, the bare deformity and shapelessness of outline of many pieces of Louis XV. Furniture is at once apparent. It is to the skill of such artists in metal as Caffieri and Gouthiere that the popularity of much of the eighteenth century Cabinet work may be attributed. Deprived of their inimitable " mounts " articles which now fetch thousands would in all probability barely fetch hundreds of pounds.

With all its faults it must also be admitted that there is great power of drawing displayed in some of the Louis XV. work—partly owing to the almost entire absence of straight lines. Bureaus, Commodes, Tables, etc., were then made shaped, not only in the front but also at the sides. They were curved in plan and also in elevation. This class of Furniture is termed "bombé." The same preponderance of shaping is to be observed in the Wardrobes, Couches, Tables, Chairs, and other articles. There was also a large amount of constructive wood-work executed in the reign of Louis XV., and many perfect examples of panelled rooms still remain to show the luxurious tastes of a frivolous but fascinating epoch. On sheet 23 are arranged several portions of Bureaux, Commodes, etc., chiefly of mahogany inlaid and mounted with ormolu ; also a variety of Chair and other legs in the same style.

As the designs of Oppenort represent the earlier Louis XV. so the work of J. A. Meissonier and François de Cuvilliés, père, may be taken as typical of the later or Rococo. Sheet 24 contains examples of both phases. The two carved frame corners at bottom of page are by Meissonier, and the carved panel at top is from a frieze in an old house in Paris built during the Regency. The centre frame dates from 1757.

Any essay on the development of the Louis Quinze style would be incomplete without reference being made to the influence exerted by Boucher and Watteau on the pictorial and industrial arts of their time. The former name is, indeed, one of the most prominent, and, although his fame in this country rests almost entirely on his skill as a painter of Cupids and pastoral scenes, he was also an efficient master of decorative design. Among the architects of the period who gave attention to Furniture, Jacqués François Blondel was probably the most talented. His great work, entitled "De la Distribution des Maisons de Plaisance et de la Decoration des Édifices en Général," which is enriched with 160 copper plates, contains some of the purest and least objectionable examples of Louis XV. design.

Although gilt wood was almost invariably used in the construction of Louis XV. Furniture there was also a large amount of lacquered work executed—much of it in imitation of the Chinese style. Robert Martin, the inventor of a varnish or lacquer bearing his name, was the most skilful practitioner in this department of art, and genuine " bits " of " Vernis Martin " are now eagerly purchased when they come under the hammer.

The Chair on plate 25 is a fine specimen of carved gilt Furniture. The covering of this chair, probably one of a set, is from the celebrated Tapestry works of Gobelin. The four corner-pieces on same sheet represent portions of Console Tables originally designed by Pinèau, who practised in the first half of the eighteenth century. This series of designs was copied by a man named Batty Langley in 1739 and published by him as his own original work—hardly an honourable transaction.

There are many difficulties in the way of an absolutely correct classification of styles, and not the least of these is when the same patterns are reproduced in various reigns. This sort of reproduction (or cribbing as some would call it) has been general at all times and the custom cannot be said to have become obsolete even yet. Numerous instances of facsimile reproductions, such as we have just alluded to, might be quoted ; but as no advantage is to be gained by exposing the malpractices of former generations, we will only draw attention to the fact, in order to account for the resemblance between many of the details here given, although belonging to different styles.

It is in transitional periods that a similarity of design is most observable, as it is obviously impossible for an artist working in two reigns to completely throw off his earlier manner immediately on the coronation of a new King. Apropos of these remarks it will be noticed that several of the mouldings on sheet 26 bear a striking resemblance to some we have given with other French styles, the enriched ones more especially. The most thoroughly characteristic Louis Quinze mouldings are irregularly curved in section. Some of these are very subtle in their delicate gradations of light and shade ; in fact, there is more in them than appears from a casual observation. While on the subject of mouldings we would impress on the designer the immense importance of this branch of his studies—it cannot, indeed, be over-rated. As it has been observed that the most necessary qualification in order to become an effective speaker is action, so it may, with equal truth, be said that a correct appreciation of the value of mouldings is of the most vital importance in order to become a good designer of Furniture or architect.

In the reign of Louis XV. brass mounts were very extensively used for the enrichment of Furniture, but specimens of separate handles for doors and drawer fronts are comparatively rare. This is partly owing to the fact that it was customary (especially in the Rococo period), to make the brass scrolls with which the drawers were ornamented, project sufficiently for them to be used as handles. Another reason for their scarcity may be ascribed to the custom of using the key itself as a handle very frequently.

In the whole of the fine collection of French Furniture at South Kensington Museum there is not a single Louis Quinze Cabinet handle of any importance, and we have been obliged to fall back upon the designs of Blondel and Cuvilliés for most of the handles, etc., on sheet 27.

In giving these examples of Louis XV. metal work, we hardly do so with the idea that they will be reproduced at the present day ; this is scarcely possible, except by means of casting from old pieces, on account of the fineness of the chasing and beauty of modelling which distinguishes the best work of this class. Such as they are, they remain to us as wonderful examples of the skill of a bygone race of artists and metal chasers, and they are interesting as illustrations of a peculiar phase of eighteenth century art, but belonging as they do essentially to the period in which they were produced, they can never be repeated with the same spirit by a generation differing so widely in character as does the Englishman of the present day from the Frenchman of the last century.

DESCRIPTION OF PLATES 23 TO 27—LOUIS XV.

PLATE

23.—Portions of Commodes, Bureaux and Chair Legs.

24.—Frieze Panel, Carved Frame, and Picture Frame Corners.

25.—Arm Chair, Corners of Four Tables, Carved Cap, Bracket and Masks.

26.—Candelabra Stand, Plain and Enriched Mouldings.

27. —Cabinet Brass Work.

LOUIS XVI.

TRICTLY speaking the term " Louis Seize " should only be applied to the Furniture, &c., which was designed during the reign of that unfortunate monarch, but such is not the case ; for many articles manufactured in the previous reign are quite Louis XVI. in character. The change of taste from the extravagances of the Rococo to the refined simplicity of Louis XVI. really commenced during the reign of Louis XV., which fact renders classification according to reign very difficult and misleading. In the illustrations of this style, only those examples have been selected which possess the true characteristics of Louis XVI. work, which may be enumerated briefly as follows : Simplicity of outline, tasteful, but sparing use of enrichment and great refinement of detail. Gilt bronze mounts, Sèvres placques, and inlays of various woods, all served to embellish the cabinets and tables of this period, and the porcelains of Wedgwood and fine lacquered panels from Japan, were also brought into requisition for the same purpose. Quivers, torches and other amourous emblems, trophies of musical instruments and swags of flowers were favourite objects of decorative treatment with the designers of this date, and we find them constantly recurring in the panels of cabinets, in the bronze mounts and in various other places, sometimes with the happiest effect. The frequent introduction of vases, tripods, masks and other antique emblems, is also characteristic of the style and may be attributed to the discoveries at Pompeii and Herculaneum towards the end of the last century.

French artists, however, were not satisfied with simply copying from the antique; they certainly borrowed old symbols, but they invariably imparted to them a French flavour, distinct and unmistakable. This antique feeling degenerated later on into the crudity and baldness of the style known as " Empire."

Among the great French cabinet makers of the Louis Seize period, the names of Riesener and Gouthière are most familiar, the former for cabinet work proper—that is the woodwork—and the latter for the highly chased mounts with which it was generally finished ; but there were also many others of almost equal excellence, such as Richter, Oeben, Pafrat, and Carlin, whose work will be admired long after their own names are forgotten. Jacquemart in his " Histoire du Mobilier," also mentions the names of Martincourt, the master of Gouthière, Delarche, Jean Louis Prieur, Vinsac and Ravrio, as having assisted in bringing the cabinet metal work of this period to the state of perfection which it ultimately attained.

The turned legs and feet arranged on plate 28 have been selected from the designs of Delafosse, Boucher, fils, Lalonde, and other contemporaneous French artists. They are intended to be finely carved and gilt, or painted white or in light tints of colour. Plate 29 shows a few of the more familiar details of the style, among which the vase plays a prominent part. We find it constantly introduced, both inlaid and carved in wood ; sometimes the vase contains flowers, and very frequently it terminates with a flame or pine cone, as shown at top of sheet 29. Shields similar to those shown on same sheet are also very common features in Louis XVI. decorations. The mouldings on plate 30 call for no special comment.

In the eighteenth century European Furniture fashions were generally derived from France ; thus we find that much of the English, German, Italian, and Spanish Cabinet work, manufactured between 1750 and 1790, was quite Louis XVI. in character. Our own "Adams'" style, which prevailed here from about 1770 to 1800, possesses many points in common with Louis XVI., though inferior to it in richness, and to go further back, Chippendale, whose book of designs was published in 1760, evidently borrowed many of his extravagant ideas from the Louis Quinze style, which was in vogue during his life. To go further back still, many, if not most, of the Queen Anne details with which we are now familiar were also derived originally from our inventive neighbours, as may be seen by comparing the productions of the two countries during Louis the XIV.'s reign.

Louis XVI. Interior Woodwork was generally of oak, painted white. The walls were divided by pilasters, either delicately carved or painted in colours ; and the mouldings were frequently gilt. The Chairs and Sofas were either covered in rich French silk or in the beautiful tapestry manufactured at Gobelins, near Paris, and Beauvais. Pastoral subjects, flowers and trophies, were worked especially for the backs and seats of chairs and settees, both singly and in sets. A complete suite of Furniture got up in this style would, it is needless to say, cost a large sum of money, and be only procurable by persons of great wealth.

Louis XVI. Cabinets and Tables, &c., were often exquisitely inlaid with woods of various colours, tulip, rosewood, pear, holly, and ebony being the most common. Blues and greens were obtained by saturating the lighter woods in chemical solutions, and by this means charming effects were produced. The pilasters and panels sketched on plate 31 have been taken from Cabinets, Screens and Armoires of the period. In these as in the other examples of this style, it will be noticed that the laurel-leaf either in the form of a wreath or swag is frequently introduced. Another feature is the use of husks in the flutes of the pilasters and legs, either dropping from the top or springing from the bottom.

The enormous prices frequently realised for good specimens of old French Furniture, may, to the uninitiated appear out of all proportion to their intrinsic value ; but when it is considered that in many instances the sums paid for them have not greatly exceeded the original cost of manufacture, these prices will not appear so disproportionate.

As an example of this expensive class of work may be mentioned the Secrétaire exhibited at Gore House in 1853, which cost originally 85,000 francs, or about £3,400, and there are many other pieces in existence whose production must have necessitated the outlay of an equally high sum. It should also be remembered that eighteenth century French Furniture, often possesses an historical interest apart from its artistic merit, through having belonged to personages who played prominent parts in an eventful period of History. Such, for instance, are the small writing-table (formerly belonging to Marie Antoinette) in the South Kensington Museum, for which the late Mr. Jones refused £5,000, and the famous secrétaire belonging to Sir Robert Wallace, which was made by Riesener, for Stanislaus, King of Poland, about 1765. Those who are only acquainted with ordinary cabinet work will be surprised to learn that to produce one of the exquisite cabinets or secrétaires just mentioned, would occupy the whole time of the most skilful workman for many years, so that in no case could such high-class work be brought within the reach of people not blessed with princely incomes. The trophies and emblematic devices on plate 32 are such as are found inlaid on cabinet fronts, &c., and some of them have been taken from carvings. They are all characterised by that light and graceful touch for which the French have long been pre-eminently remarkable. The cabinet brass-work of this time is beyond all praise. The sketches on sheet 33 may give a general idea of the design, but it is impossible in a mere pen and ink sketch, to reproduce the extreme delicacy and daintiness of the best work executed during this period, by Gouthière and his contemporaries—almost equalling in finish the productions of the goldsmith or jeweller. The handles, &c., on plate 33 have been taken from examples in private collections and from the Jones collection previously mentioned.

In concluding this brief résumé of a fascinating period of French art, one cannot do better than quote a paragraph from Jacquemart's " Histoire du Mobilier," an English translation of which is to be obtained. He remarks : " Under Louis XVI., the period of refinement of every description, wood was to enter on a new phase ; not only its forms are sobered down by being covered with delicate details, but it carries coquetry to the extent of abandoning gold decoration to show itself clothed in a simple coating of white paint, barely relieved in some cases by mouldings of pale lilac or sky-blue. Nothing can be prettier than a little drawing-room in this style, in which the borders of the glasses, sometimes surmounted by an amorous trophy with its doves and torch, the console tables with white marble tops, furniture in pale figured satin, or in striped silk with soft tints, have no other relief but the fine ornamented bronzes as delicate as jewelry, thus permitting the beauty and elegance of the ladies who inhabited them, and enlivened them by their animated grace to appear unrivalled. It must be admitted that this much abused eighteenth century had, in its latter days, discovered the secret of the most refined taste, and the highest degree of politeness and ' bon ton.' "

DESCRIPTION OF PLATES 28 TO 33—LOUIS XVI.

PLATE.

28.—Table and Chair, Legs.

29.—Vases, Shields and Brackets.

30.—Mouldings.

31.—Pilasters and Panels.

32.—Trophies.

33.—Cabinet Brass Work.

"SHERATON."

HE three English Cabinet-makers of the last century whose names are most familiar to the present generation, are Thos. Chippendale, A. Heppelwhite, and Thos. Sheraton. The first named, by reason probably, of the greater importance of his published designs, is the most celebrated, and in many instances the productions of other makers are erroneously attributed to him. As the chief characteristics of Chippendale Furniture are very generally known, and there is a marked decline in the popularity of that style of Cabinet work, it has not been thought necessary to reproduce its familiar details here. Many of these are open to strong objections on the score of bad taste ; although the execution of the Cabinet work and carving is, in most instances, excellent. Chippendale's principal pattern book was published in 1764. Next in rotation comes Heppelwhite, who, in 1789, issued an important set of designs for Household Furniture of every description. Most of the articles he represents are very graceful and were it not for the extreme rarity of the volume, Heppelwhite would, no doubt, have achieved a more widespread reputation. It is probable that Sheraton was acquainted with his drawings, for there is a marked resemblance between many of the designs of the two makers. Sheraton's first and best work, entitled the "Cabinet-Makers' and Upholsterers' Drawing Book," was issued in 1791. It contains numerous patterns for Sideboards, Tables, Beds, Chairs, Fire Screens, Knife Cases, Secretaires, Dressing Tables, Tripods, etc., etc. A refined treatment is adopted throughout ; the tendency being rather towards simplicity than over-enrichment. The workmanship displayed in those pieces which have come down to us at the present day is as nearly perfect as possible ; in fact, were it not for want of polish or rough usage, many of the articles would be as sound and serviceable now as they were the day they left the workshop. Plates 34, 35, and 36 will give some idea of the style of Sheraton's designs. On sheet 34 are grouped a small Secretary or Writing Cabinet, two Chair Backs and various Cornice Mouldings. The Secretary is intended to be made of satinwood, cross banded, with a brass gallery at top, and the small swag drapery at back of glass doors should be of silk. Plate 35 shows a Sideboard, two Bookcase Doors and two Table Legs, etc., mostly taken from the "Cabinet-Makers' and Upholsterers' Drawing Book" just mentioned. Sheraton Sideboards were generally made without backs. The usual mode of finishing them (when the tops were not left perfectly plain) was with two horizontal brass rods fixed to uprights, also of brass, and occasionally with Candelabra springing from the centre or from the ends. (See plate 35.) Occasionally a Convex Mirror was attached to the rods by means of brass scrolls, but this was the exception rather than the rule. The two legs represented on same sheet belong to Card or Side Tables. The carving on these, as on most of the Furniture of Sheraton's time, would be finely executed in dark Spanish mahogany, the tops of the articles, drawer fronts and panels, being generally relieved with bands of satinwood. From the numerous patterns of Glazed Cabinet and Bookcase Doors shown in the " Drawing Book " two have been selected which are rather less common than the majority of patterns in general use. The figure on centre panel of left-hand door would be painted.

Sheet 36 comprises a Bookcase Pediment, a small Cabinet (very light and graceful) a pretty Ladies' Writing Table and an Enclosed Work Table. All these articles, although simple in construction, show an intimate acquaintance, on the part of their designer, with the requirements of the people for whom they were intended. Sheraton, besides being a first-rate Cabinet-maker was also possessed of considerable mechanical talent. This is evidenced by the many ingenious arrangements described in his book for opening and closing washstand and writing-table tops and the cylinder fronts of writing-tables and the revolving and other apparatus for bookcases ; all of which were made objects of careful study and wrought out with much ingenuity by this conscientious old Cabinet-maker. It is the possession of the sound qualities we have mentioned, with the addition of a considerable amount of taste, that makes Sheraton Furniture still popular. It may not be attractive or showy at first sight but it improves on acquaintance and will bear close examination—the interior fittings being quite equal, in point of workmanship to the exterior.

Among other characteristic articles in use at this time were the Knife Boxes. These were generally made in pairs and stood on the sideboards. Much care was often lavished on these small articles. It is not unusual to meet with them elaborately painted or inlaid and mounted with handsome ornamental lock plates.

DESCRIPTION OF PLATES 34, 35, 36—SHERATON.

PLATE

34.—Satinwood Writing Cabinet, Two Carved Chair Backs, and Cornice Mouldings.

35.—Cornice of Bookcase, Two Table Legs, Inlaid Sideboard, Mahogany Vase, and Two Bookcase Doors.

36.—Pediment for Bookcase or Wardrobe, Satinwood Cabinet, with Inlaid and Painted Panels, Small Satinwood Writing Table and Mahogany Work Table.

"ADABS."

EW Architects or Furniture designers have been gifted with sufficient
originality to permanently identify their names with the styles they
invented. Among the notable exceptions to this rule, are Chippendale,
Sheraton, and Adams in England, and Boule in France. There certainly
were the brothers Martin, who manufactured decorative Furniture in Paris
in the latter half of the last century, and coated it with a very fine varnish similar
in many respects to Japanese lacquer; but their name can hardly be given to the
Furniture itself. It was more in connection with the finish of the surface that they
displayed their skill and originality. "Vernis Martin Furniture" would not be so
highly prized were it not for the taste displayed in its decoration. Figure subjects,
and landscapes with figures "a la Watteau," were introduced in the panels and flat
surfaces of the tables, commodes, etc., with charming effect on grounds possessing a
metallic lustre, and the whole of the article was afterwards coated with a very hard
lacquer which not only preserved the painting, but imparted an additional value to
the enrichments.

With Chippendale and Sheraton Furniture we are all tolerably familiar, owing to
the numerous reproductions of old pieces by those celebrated makers, but with regard
to "Adams" some uncertainty seems to prevail. This may partly be accounted for
by reason of the scarcity of authentic designs for Furniture by Robert and James
Adams accessible to the general public. It is true there are several sheets of
Furniture included in the large Architectural work by Adams, but this book is so
very costly, that it does not often come under the notice of Cabinet-makers.

As the name is so often mentioned in connection with Architecture and Furnishing
it may be interesting to those who are not acquainted with the history of the
"Adelphi Brothers" to give a few particulars relating to their early career.

Robert Adams, the most talented of the family, was born in Edinburgh in 1728.
He developed a taste for drawing at a very early age, and continued to cultivate it with
a view to becoming a landscape artist. For this purpose he made a journey to Italy,
and there is very little doubt that his sojourn in that country—so full of Architectural
beauties—made a lasting impression on his mind and gave that bent to his genius
which subsequently earned for him a well-deserved reputation. It was during his
residence abroad that he conceived the idea of publishing a series of reproductions of

careful drawings made by himself of the ruins of the Emperor Diocletian's palace at Spalatio, a plan which he carried into effect on his return to England, and on completion of the book, which was far in advance of any Architectural work that had previously appeared in this country, he dedicated it to King George III. This at once established his reputation, and he was shortly after appointed Architect to his majesty.

His industry must have been unflagging, for he not only erected mansions and public buildings all over the country and in Scotland, but designed the Decorations, Furniture, and even the carpets for the various apartments. He is best known to the present generation by the three magnificent volumes (" Works in Architecture ") published between 1778 and 1822 ; but these only contain a small portion of his designs. A large collection of original drawings by Robert and James Adams is preserved in the Library of Soane's Museum, Lincoln's Inn Fields, where they have lain many years in comparative obscurity. They were no doubt purchased by Sir John Soane, who was himself an architect of some note, shortly after Adams's death.

Of James Adams, it may be said, that whatever merit he possessed may be attributed to the influence and example of his brother. It is quite certain that Robert Adams must have had a very large number of clever assistants, or he could never have carried out the enormous amount of work which he is known to have been directly responsible for. The strong individuality of the man is proved by the fact that the whole of the Architecture, Furniture, Silver Plate and even the domestic utensils of his time are stamped indelibly with the style he invented. Whatever its faults may be with regard to want of vigour and originality—it was undoubtedly an improvement on the class of work that preceded it. Its popularity, even at the present day says much in its favour, also the fact that it has always been a favourite style with people of refined tastes.

A cursory glance at the Furniture Designs by Adams preserved in Soane's Museum, is sufficient to show that he had a marked preference for colour as a method of Decoration for Cabinet work. Of the designs above mentioned, the majority are drawn to a large scale in pen and ink, and afterwards carefully finished in various tints. Nearly all of them are carried out in this way, the few remaining examples being gilt work. These remarks apply strictly to the Cabinet Furniture, not to the Girandoles, Glasses, Wall lights, Frames, etc., which were generally gilt, although even in these articles, colour was often introduced by him. The favourite details with Adams were the vase, with husks swags, delicate scrolls, fan-shaped ornaments, flutes and pateræ and oval and circular medallions containing classical figures in the style of Angelica Kaufmann and Cipriani. The lines of his ornament are invariably graceful, although it is sometimes too attenuated for its position, but when the enrichment is sufficiently near the eye to be appreciated, no fault can be found.

The few examples of "Adams Furniture" given on plates 37, 38, 39, are sufficient to show how much the effect depends on the painted enrichments. Constructively it is very simple, having been made so, apparently, in order to afford plenty of scope for the brush of the decorator who, it must be admitted, often gave considerable interest and beauty to articles which would otherwise have had only a plain and boxy appearance. The small Cabinet, half of which is shown on plate 37 would be absolutely uninteresting were it not for the surface decorations on doors and frieze and the chair back on same sheet owes its attraction to the same appropriate treatment of its flat surfaces. The two Caps on plate 37 are not, strictly speaking, furniture details, but as they are likely to be useful to the Designer of interiors they have been introduced here. The larger of the two is especially good. It is intended to be executed in stone, but similar Caps to this are to be found of wood in " Adams " Chimney pieces. Many of the " Adams " Chimney pieces were mounted with composition and afterwards tinted.

Plate 38 includes a bow-fronted satinwood Cabinet with painted panels, two window Cornices from the Soane Collection intended for treatment in colours ; the upper corner of a bookcase from the same source, and a portion of an overdoor from a house at the West End of London. The trellis-work in front of bookcase door is of brass.

The examples on plate 39 are from the "Works in Architecture" above mentioned. The centre piece represents the upper portion of a carved and gilt console glass. The table legs, brackets, and pedestal are of carved wood also.

DESCRIPTION OF PLATES 37, 38, 39.

PLATE

37.—Painted Cabinet and Chair back, End of Seat, and two " Adams' " Caps.

38.—Satinwood Painted Cabinet, two Cornices, Portion of Bookcase and Overdoor.

39.—Top of Pier Glass, Carved Wood, four Legs, Pedestal and Brackets.

" EMPIRE."

THE old pieces of Furniture preserved in our Museums and public galleries are the most faithful records we possess of the habits and customs of bygone generations, and, as such, are of immense value to the historian, the antiquary, and the artist. In the few examples already given in this series, we can see in turn how the grandeur of Louis XIVth's time gradually degenerated into the extravagance and meaningless frivolity which characterised the reign of his successor, and how truer principles of art revived again in the graceful style of Louis Seize. Were it necessary to express the characteristics of the three reigns in equally few words, Grandeur, Frivolity, and Prettiness, (each evidenced in the Furniture) would with tolerable correctness describe them.

We come now to a different style altogether. The selfish luxury of the nobility of France at the end of the eighteenth century, sustained through many weary years at the expense of the working classes, at last bore natural fruit in the horrors of a revolution. At the commencement of that frightful period, the genius of Art, terror stricken, spread her wings and flew away to more peaceful scenes, returning again only when the blood had dried up in the streets of Paris. But what a change had taken place during that brief absence! Whereas formerly all was luxury, "abandon" and pleasure in its most polished and attractive guise, now everything was severe, emotionless, hard, and unnatural. It was then the Empire reaction had set in, and the excess of licence gave place to the excess of Austerity, in outward appearance at any rate.

It was the "falsehood of extremes" in both instances, for neither the follies of the Louis Quinze régime, nor the severities of the Empire, truly represented the French nature, they only reflected popular feeling at two remarkable periods of the country's history. Similar waves of public sentiment have passed over this country, notably during the Commonwealth, and the reaction in an opposite direction in Charles the Second's time.

To return to our immediate subject, viz., Empire Furniture. This, like the Art and Manners of the time, was unnatural, from the fact that the designs for it were appropriated from others that had been invented by the Greeks and Romans under entirely different states of society, hundreds of years before. Chairs, Tables, Tripods, Couches, &c., were copied almost in facsimile from old Greek vases and wall decorations, and even the dress of the period had a severe classical appearance. To increase the general "penchant" of the time for classic forms, David, an artist of considerable talent and influence, painted pictures in the modern-antique fashion; and the designs Percier and Fontaine, Fragonard, fils, and others, still further fostered the taste, and crystallized the then chaotic state of ornamental design into something that could be denominated a Style, which despite its lack of originality—subsequently invaded Europe. It was in France, however, that the best examples were produced. Whatever may have been the sins of omission or commission that may be attributed to the Emperor Napoleon I., that of neglecting the Decorative arts, cannot be included ; for the French palaces and public buildings of the time bear ample evidence to the contrary; being full of remains of this interesting epoch. It is not necessary, however, for Londoners who wish to gain an idea of "Empire" Furniture to go so far, as Madame Tussaud's Exhibition in Baker Street includes many fine specimens, also candelabra, paintings, &c. These were acquired, we believe, with other Napoleon relics, by the late Madame Tussaud, after Napoleon's final defeat early in the present century.

As in all other French styles, "Empire" was closely imitated in this country. Its chief merit consists in the extreme nicety of finish exhibited in the metal work, which was very extensively used, both for the enrichment of furniture, and also for clocks, vases, candlesticks, inkstands, &c. As an example of finish, the metal work of this date is admirable, and the figures when introduced are generally well drawn, although they have the hardness peculiar to the time.

It is impossible to have a better authority on "Empire" Furniture, than the book of designs published in Paris, by the architects, Percier and Fontaine, in 1809. This work is the recognised text-book of the period, and a great point in its favour is the fact that all the objects represented have been actually carried out, so that they are not mere exercises of fancy, as is often the case with publications of a similar character. Most of the examples of this style we have given on plates, 40, 41, and 42 have been derived from the above work, and in justice to these able architects, we must mention, that in the preface to their Book, they disclaim all credit on the score of originality, and frankly admit they are indebted solely to the antique for their inspirations.

This shows the modesty of true artists, which they certainly were ; and although their designs may not lay claim to novelty of detail, no unprejudiced person will be inclined to deny that considerable taste and ingenuity, and a vast amount of learned research was necessary in order to adapt the beautiful remains of antiquity to modern requirements. This they undoubtedly did in a masterly manner, and their productions, if nothing else, remain a mute but eloquent protest against the slovenly execution of much of the industrial art of the present day. All they did was carried out *con amore ;* they were enthusiasts evidently, and bestowed the most careful attention on points of comparatively small importance. It is impossible to give a fair idea of the high finish of Empire Cabinet work in a small sketch. It must be seen to be properly appreciated.

Plate 40 includes several tables, seats and chairs, in the above style. These would be made of dark mahogany, with water-gilt metal mounts, finely chased. The commodes and centre table on plate 41, are from Percier and Fontaine's designs. The upper piece is described by them as having drawers enclosed with two doors, mounted with bronze and mother-o'-pearl. In the lower commode, the drawers come to the front. Both of these are very chaste in conception. The idea for the centre table was derived from antique fragments of a similar article preserved in the museum of the Vatican.

On plate 42 are represented a candelabrum, a secretaire, a small work table, a "Table-de-nuit" or bedside pedestal, and an arm chair from the same source. The candelabrum is of wood, carved and gilt. The secretaire is described as being of various woods, mounted with bronze plaques. In the upper portion is a clock face, surrounded with the signs of the zodiac, and under it are secret drawers; the cylinder when raised discloses the writing apparatus, and at each side are chimerical figures supporting lights.

The work-table and commode are also of wood with bronze mounts, and the chair would be made *en suite*.

DESCRIPTION OF PLATES 40, 41, 42.—"EMPIRE."
PLATE

CHINESE.

LTHOUGH the industrial arts were practised in China at a very early period, very little, if any, progress appears to have been made within our knowledge ; and, on the other hand, there seems to have been no perceptible deterioration in the quality of their work. The carving, the Furniture, the porcelain, and the embroidery recently executed will bear favourable comparison with that turned out a hundred, two hundred, or five hundred years ago—it is no better and no worse. The designs, even, of the various objects and patterns now in use are almost precisely similar to the older ones. To what are we to attribute this stationary position of the Arts, so unparalleled in history ? The only reasonable explanation is that the Chinese, as a nation, reached the limit of their artistic powers centuries ago, and, in the absence of all foreign intercourse whatever, they have exhausted their own ideas, and, instead of attempting to invent new types, they fall back on the time-honoured patterns that satisfied their ancestors.

Chinese design shows very little invention. When the ornament is not of a simple geometrical character, it generally takes a floral form, interwoven or bound together with straight or fretted lines. The wood construction is of an equally primitive character, and can hardly be dignified with the appellation of style, as we understand it. The term is used for want of a better. Most of the examples on sheets 43 and 44 have been reproduced from Sir William Chambers' Chinese sketches, taken in Canton, and afterwards published in this country. They are authentic examples, and, although ancient, will give a very correct idea of the ordinary Furniture used in China at the present day, as a hundred odd years count for very little in the Flowery Land. At the same time, we cannot do better than quote Sir William Chambers' own description of Chinese interiors, as seen by him during his sojourn in that interesting country. He says : " The moveables of the saloon consist of chairs, stools, and tables ; made sometimes of rosewood, ebony, or lacquered work, and sometimes of bamboo only, which is cheap, and, nevertheless, very neat. When the moveables are of wood, the seats of the stools are often of marble or porcelain, which, though hard to sit on, are far from unpleasant in a climate where the summer heats are excessive. In the corners of the rooms are stands 4 or 5 feet high, on which they set plates of citrons, and other fragrant fruits, or branches of coral in vases of porcelain, and glass globes containing gold-fish, together with a certain weed somewhat resembling fennel ; on such tables as are intended for ornament only they also place little landscapes, composed of rocks, shrubs, and a kind of lily that grows among pebbles covered with water. Sometimes, also, they have artificial landscapes made of ivory, crystal, amber, pearls, and various stones. I have seen some of these that cost above 300 guineas, but they are at best mere baubles, and miserable imitations of nature. Besides these landscapes, they adorn their tables with several vases of porcelain, and little vessels of copper, which are held in great esteem. These are generally of simple and pleasing forms. The Chinese say they were made two thousand years ago by some of their celebrated artists and such as are real antiques (for there are many counterfeits) they buy at an extravagant price, giving sometimes no less than £300 sterling for one of them.

" The bedroom is divided from the saloon by a partition of folding doors, which, when the weather is hot, are in the night thrown open to admit the air. It is very small, and contains no other furniture than the bed, and some varnished chests in which they keep their apparel. The beds are very magnificent; the bedsteads are made much like ours in Europe—of rosewood, carved, or lacquered work; the curtains are of taffeta or gauze, sometimes flowered with gold, and commonly either blue or purple. About the top a slip of white satin, a foot in breadth, runs all round, on which are painted, in panels, different figures—flower pieces, landscapes, and conversation pieces, interspersed with moral sentences and fables written in Indian ink and vermilion."

Our readers will recognise many of the articles here described on sheets 43 and 44 of this series.

Wood being the principal material used by the Chinese in their architecture as well as their Furniture, it is not surprising that they should have attained considerable skill in its manipulation. The houses, temples, porticoes, and bridges, are chiefly of timber, sometimes very ornately carved. As a rule the harder descriptions of wood are selected for furniture, such as harewood, ebony, or teak; bamboo and cane being used for the lighter articles. The Chinese have always been very partial to perforated work (fretwork, as we now call it); they also frequently introduce in the panels of the Furniture and Chair-backs, intricate and fantastically-carved open work patterns.

The beauty of Chinese and Japanese lacquer is universally known. It is used as a finish for every description of wood construction by the natives of both those countries; and although many attempts have been made to discover the secret of its manufacture and application, hitherto all such experiments have failed. The Chinese style has been popular in Europe, off and on, for nearly two hundred years; and it will always have a certain number of admirers, on account of its quaintness and individuality.

DESCRIPTION OF PLATES 43 AND 44.—CHINESE.

PLATE

43.—Two Pedestals, Seat, Portion of Bedstead, Corners of two Tables, Fret-cut Panels, and Carved Stand.

44.—Bamboo Chair, Portion of Settee, three Tables, Pedestal, and Fret Patterns.

JAPANESE.

THE enormous importation of Japanese goods into England during the last few years, has resulted in a very general knowledge of the Arts of that interesting country. Lacquered Cabinets, Trays, Screens, Nests of Drawers, Fans, Lanterns, China and Ornamental Bronzes, of more or less good design and colouring, are to be met with all over the country, and the wonder is that a territory of such comparatively small dimensions, should, after retaining sufficient for its own requirements, be able to export such an enormous quantity of artistic objects to Europe and America. Much has been written of the Art instincts of the Japanese. Judging from what is to be seen in London alone, their fine perception of form and eye for colour, have not been in the least over-rated. A want of appreciation for Art must, in Japan, be the exception rather than the rule. It needs only a cursory glance at any group of Japanese objects, to become impressed with the fact that they are patient and faithful admirers of Nature in all its phases. Their studies of flowers, birds on the wing and in every conceivable position, fish, and even insects, are simply marvellous ; but Japanese Art is a topic on which so much has been written, and on which one could enthusiastically enlarge to such an extent that I am compelled, owing to the limited scope of these descriptive papers, to restrict myself to the consideration of Japanese Furniture and Woodwork, with which we are more immediately concerned.

The Japanese style, although possessing many points of resemblance to the Chinese, is if anything, more eccentric, and the decorative portions are less conventional. Of old Japanese Furniture, there is very little. Chairs appear to have been considered unnecessary until quite lately, the people generally preferring to sit on the floor ; consequently high tables were also of very little use. Now, however, as they have adopted that crowning triumph of civilization, the "stove pipe" hat, they will no doubt also begin to use chairs; for a venerable Japanese official seated on the floor with a high hat on would certainly fail to impress beholders with the same sense of reverence as if that dignitary were seated on a chair.

For the convenience of those occupying the lowly position we have described, small tables or stands varying from 9 to 18 inches in height are provided. Three of these are represented on plate 45. These would be made of ebony or lacquered. The small cabinet at top of sheet, though only one of the ordinary articles produced for export, has many features deserving attention. Such comparatively unimportant details as hinges, lock plates, and mounts, are here wrought out with much care and

K

taste, forming in themselves the chief decorative portions of the cabinet. Three of these mounts are represented enlarged to nearly full size. The centre of screen on same sheet is formed of jointed wood, and the birds and flowers in side compartments are produced by piercing a thin panel with a fine saw or chisel. Of Japanese Screens there are endless varieties, varying as much in design as in pecuniary value. It is possible to get a very pretty and serviceable three-fold screen, hand-painted, for about 25s., and some of them fetch as much as £1,000 each.

They are sometimes filled with embroidered silk panels, and they are also carved and inlaid with mother-o'-pearl and various coloured stones, lacquered, painted, and incised.

There is one fact which cannot fail to impress itself on those who are acquainted with the Furniture of the Japanese, viz. : that although the articles may vary to an almost unlimited extent in costliness of material and elaboration of detail, the general types of construction remain the same. The Cabinets or Screens costing a few shillings are of the same build as those costing many pounds. This is not the case with European Furniture. Like the Chinese—the Japanese have been until the present century a conservative nation, but with the spread of European culture and the adoption of English institutions, there has arisen a desire to imitate European models and graft on them the native decorations of the country, the result being a hybrid production, devoid of artistic merit. This course, if persisted in, will be disastrous in the extreme and fatal to the Arts of Japan.

Sheet 46 contains a small lacquered open Cabinet, a low stand of carved wood, a Nest of Drawers with arrangement on top, apparently intended for the uses of the toilet, which by the way is often performed on the floor ; a lacquered Cabinet, mounted with small china placques and the usual elaborate key plates, hinges, &c., and two carved paterae.

Bamboo, Cane, Coloured Stones, Pearl, and Metals of every description are pressed into service by the Japanese Cabinet-makers. Nothing comes amiss to them and the different substances are generally introduced in those positions where the most original and appropriate effects will be produced. For instance, coloured stones are selected to represent the various tints of flowers and leaves and the feathers on the wings of birds, fruit, vegetables, &c. Pearl is used for imitating shells and water, and gold and silver for other objects. The large Cabinet at top of sheet 47 has been sketched from one in the South Kensington Museum. It is formed of matted cane on a foundation of wood, the base being of wood, carved and coloured red.

The flowers and other ornaments are of coloured cane. This cabinet is about 7-ft. high, and 6-ft. 6-in. wide. The small table on same sheet is of ebonized wood, and the panels at sides are inlaid.

DESCRIPTION OF PLATES 45, 46, 47—JAPANESE.

PLATE

45.—Lacquered Cabinet, with White Metal Mounts, Perforated Screen, Three Small Tables, and Carved Panel.

46.—Four-Tier Table, Dressing Box, Carved Stand, Lacquered Cabinet, with China Placques in Panels, Two Carved Paterae.

47.—Cabinet of Matted Cane, Ebony Table, and Two Inlaid Panels.

ARABIAN.

HE earliest specimens of Arabian Architecture were founded on the Roman and Byzantine buildings which they displaced. The general forms and proportions of the earlier structures were, to a limited extent, retained, and the ornamental details were adapted by the Arabs to the new conditions of life and religion. Traces of the Byzantine influence may be readily observed in early Arabian work; but, as the style developed, the original "motifs" entirely disappear.

Specimens of Arabian Furniture are not common. This is partly owing to the scarcity of wood in that part of Asia and also to the fact that comparatively few articles are considered necessary in the furnishing of an Arab apartment. Of constructive wood-work in the shape of Screens, Doors, Projecting Windows and Balustrades, there are endless examples, both in Arabia and in this country, a demand having sprung up during the last few years for "Cairene" fitments which has been promptly met by the native craftsmen.

The Arabs have always been particularly clever at the elaborate interlacing of mouldings in the form of Panels of various geometrical designs. Some of their exterior and interior doors of this description are marvels of construction. They are also very partial to Lattice Work made up of small turned spindles and cubes of wood. (See plates 48 and 49).

Arab Furniture consists chiefly of comfortable Seats or Divans, generally ranged round the room, Wooden Benches with open-work backs and foot rests (such as are shown on plate 48), Octagon or Round Tables, sometimes carved and inlaid, and fixed or hanging Cabinets with a variety of little openings for ornaments. These Cabinets are often painted and decorated in gold and colours.

The portion of interior balcony at top left-hand corner of plate 48 has been taken from the sumptuous work by M. Prisse d'Avennes, entitled "L'Art Arabe," a book that should be studied by everyone who wishes to gain a thorough knowledge of Arabian Art. The seat with cushions on same sheet is from a Barber's Shop, after Coste, restored. On plate 49 are shown a portion of a Projecting Balcony from Cairo, dating from the seventeenth century, at present fixed in one of the Furniture Courts at South Kensington Museum, a Panelled and Painted Door from the same source, a Battlemented Ornament from the work of M. Prisse d'Avennes, already alluded to, and a Small Octagon Table and Two Caps from other sources.

The somewhat elaborate specimen of Cabinet-work represented at top of page 50 is a portion of the back of a throne or seat, similar to those used by the Arabs, according to the authority of M. d'Avennes, in their sleeping apartments. The upper portion of this seat is surmounted with a canopy and there is a foot-stool attached to the lower part, similar to the one shown on plate 48. The enrichments on this seat consist of mother-o'-pearl and ivory. The Small Cabinet shown below (page 50) is a very interesting example of the class of painted Furniture previously mentioned. Although fitted Cabinets of a similar design are not uncommon, separate pieces are very rarely met with. The decorations on this Cabinet are executed in gold and colours, but unfortunately, owing to the nature of the pigments used or from some other cause, portions of the beautiful Arabesque ornamentations are peeling off. The Cabinet from which the sketch was taken is in the collection of a gentleman at Bayswater.

DESCRIPTION OF PLATES 48, 49, 50—ARABIAN.

PLATE

48.—Interior Balcony, Two Window Heads, Fitted Seat, Seat with Footstool, Arabesque Ornament, Fret Patterns.

49.—Portion of Balcony, Panelled Door, Two Caps, Small Table, and Ornamental Details.

50.—Back of Seat, inlaid with Mother-o'-Pearl and Ivory, Small Painted and Gilt Cabinet, Two Borders.